Searchlight BOOKS™

DISCARD

How Does Government Work?

Documents of Freedom

A Look at the Declaration of Independence, the Bill of Rights, and the U.S. Constitution

Gwenyth Swain

Lerner Publications Company
Minneapolis

Lerner Publications Company
A division of Lerner Publishing Group, Inc.
241 First Avenue North
Minneapolis, MN 55401 U.S.A.

Website address: www.lernerbooks.com

Library of Congress Cataloging-in-Publication Data

Swain, Gwenyth, 1961–
    Documents of freedom : a look at the Declaration of Independence, the Bill of Rights, and the U.S. Constitution / by Gwenyth Swain.
        p.   cm. — (Searchlight books™—How does government work?)
    Includes index.
    ISBN 978-0-7613-6514-3 (lib. bdg. : alk. paper)
    1. United States. Declaration of Independence—Juvenile literature. 2. United States. Constitution—Juvenile literature. 3. United States. Constitution. 1st–10th Amendments—Juvenile literature. 4. United States—Politics and government—1775–1783—Juvenile literature. 5. United States—Politics and government—1783–1789—Juvenile literature. I. Title.
E221.S94 2012
973.3'13—dc22   2010041922

Manufactured in the United States of America
1 – DP – 12/31/11

Contents

Chapter 1

SEEKING FREEDOM

In the 1600s, people from Europe settled on the eastern coast of North America. Their settlements were called colonies.

Settlers from Europe build a home and carry supplies to shore in this drawing. What were the Europeans' settlements called?

For many years, Great Britain and its king ruled the thirteen colonies set up in North America. That meant people in these colonies had to obey Britain's laws.

By the mid-1700s, many colonists had grown tired of obeying Britain. They didn't like Britain's king, George III. The colonists had come to America to find freedom. But they had to obey the king whether they liked it or not.

King George III ruled Britain from 1760 to 1820. He also ruled the colonies in North America.

The part of Britain's government that makes laws is called Parliament. Colonists also had to obey Parliament. People in Britain had to obey Parliament too. But they could vote for Parliament's members. The colonists couldn't.

This painting shows Parliament meeting in the early 1700s.

Stamp Act

In 1765, Parliament passed the Stamp Act. This law said colonists had to pay a tax on paper goods. The Stamp Act angered the colonists. They protested. In 1766, Parliament ended the law.

People in New York protest the Stamp Act by burning paper goods.

Tea Tax

Colonists rejoiced. But not for long. A tax on tea followed. The colonists protested this tax too. In 1773, some of them threw tea in the harbor of Boston, Massachusetts. They chose to throw away the tea rather than pay the tax.

Colonists in Boston protested the tea tax by dumping tea in the harbor. They dressed like Native Americans to hide who they were.

In 1774, Parliament passed laws to punish colonists. Boston Harbor was closed until colonists paid for the tea they'd thrown in the water. British soldiers marched through Boston's streets. Colonists had to let the soldiers eat and sleep in their homes.

British soldiers stay in a colonist's home against his will.

Time for Change

Colonists grew so angry that they sent leaders from each colony to a meeting. It was called the Continental Congress. It took place in Pennsylvania in 1774. At the meeting, the leaders talked about what to do.

This drawing from 1783 shows the Continental Congress meeting in 1774.

Colonists get ready to fight back by taking weapons from British troops in New York in 1775.

Most colonists still hoped to get along with Britain. But in 1775, more British troops came to the colonies. Some colonists thought war might break out. They decided to get ready to fight.

No one knows who fired the first shots in Lexington and Concord. But in those Massachusetts towns, both colonists and British troops died. King George said what most colonists already knew. The Americans were in rebellion, or an armed fight, against him.

The Battle of Lexington took place on April 19, 1775.

Still, most colonists didn't want to break away from Britain. They just wanted the taxes to end. But in 1776, a writer named Thomas Paine wrote a pamphlet called *Common Sense*. It called for independence, or self-rule.

The pamphlet changed the colonists' views. In the summer of 1776, colonial leaders made a declaration about independence. And they made history too.

COMMON SENSE;

ADDRESSED TO THE

INHABITANTS

OF

AMERICA,

On the following interesting

SUBJECTS.

I. Of the Origin and Design of Government in general, with concise Remarks on the English Constitution.

II. Of Monarchy and Hereditary Succession.

III. Thoughts on the present State of American Affairs.

IV. Of the present Ability of America, with some miscellaneous Reflections.

Man knows no Master save creating HEAVEN,
Or those whom choice and common good ordain.
THOMSON.

PHILADELPHIA;
Printed, and Sold, by R. BELL, in Third-Street.
MDCCLXXVI.

Thomas Paine wrote *Common Sense* in 1776. It encouraged the colonists to seek independence.

Chapter 2

THE DECLARATION OF INDEPENDENCE

Thomas Jefferson of Virginia didn't want to be in Philadelphia in the summer of 1776. The weather was muggy and hot. But a meeting was taking place there. It was the Second Continental Congress.

Thomas Jefferson traveled many miles to the Second Continental Congress. Where was this meeting held?

Jefferson was a delegate at the meeting. That meant he was one of the people speaking there. He was speaking for the Virginia colony.

A DELEGATE ADDRESSES THE SECOND CONTINENTAL CONGRESS IN 1776.

Lee's Motion

In June 1776, Richard Henry Lee (another delegate) made a motion. A motion is a formal statement. Lee said the colonies should be independent states. Those at the meeting talked about the motion. Should they support it? Or should they make peace with Britain?

Richard Henry Lee was also a delegate from Virginia.

A Committee

The men couldn't decide. They set up a committee to talk some more. Jefferson was on the committee. So were Benjamin Franklin, Roger Sherman, Robert R. Livingston, and John Adams.

This drawing shows the committee made up of (FROM LEFT) **Thomas Jefferson, Roger Sherman, Benjamin Franklin, Robert R. Livingston, and John Adams.**

By the middle of 1776, the committee decided they supported independence. They asked Jefferson to draft a declaration of independence. On June 28, he had a draft ready.

At the same time, other colonists were still fighting Britain. They'd formed an army under General George Washington. A full-blown war was taking place. It was the Revolutionary War (1775–1783).

Thomas Jefferson reads a rough draft of the Declaration of Independence to Benjamin Franklin.

Final Document

The declaration would have to take a backseat to the war. Still, those at the meeting took their job seriously. They worked with Jefferson's draft until it was a final document.

The final document says good government gets its power from the people. And it says the people should be free. The document became the Declaration of Independence on July 4, 1776.

The Declaration of Independence was printed and sent to Britain and throughout the colonies.

Treaty

Seven years of war followed the approval of the Declaration. In 1783, Britain lost the war. Both sides signed a treaty. This agreement said the colonies no longer belonged to Britain. They were free to become the United States.

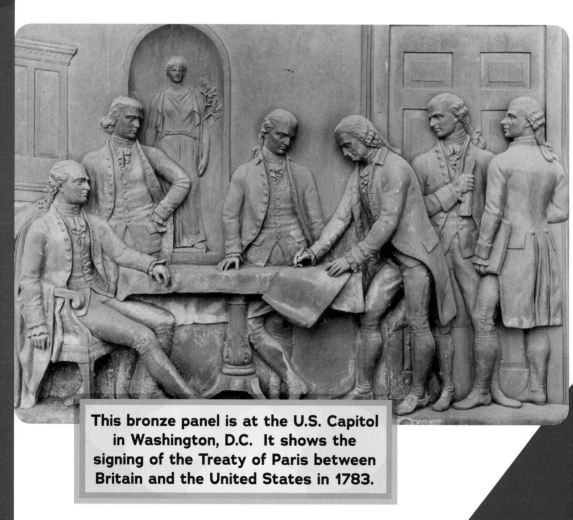

This bronze panel is at the U.S. Capitol in Washington, D.C. It shows the signing of the Treaty of Paris between Britain and the United States in 1783.

Chapter 3

THE CONSTITUTION

This is the first of two pages in the Articles of Confederation. In what year was this document written?

U.S. problems weren't over after the country won freedom. The government was a mess. The government's powers were outlined in the Articles of Confederation. This document was written in 1777. It was approved in 1781. But under the Articles, the thirteen states didn't act much like the United States. They acted like separate countries.

Good Idea

In 1786, a Virginian named James Madison had an idea. Why not send delegates to Philadelphia to rewrite the Articles of Confederation? Almost everyone agreed with this idea. The delegates' meeting was planned for the next year.

JAMES MADISON LATER BECAME THE FOURTH PRESIDENT OF THE UNITED STATES.

New Plan

Madison worked hard to prepare for the meeting. It was called the Constitutional Convention. Madison and other Virginians wrote a plan for changing the Articles. They called it the Virginia Plan.

The plan said the country should share one president. It said the country should have one Congress. This would be a lawmaking body made up of people from each state. The plan also said Congress should have two parts. Those parts would be called the Senate and the House of Representatives.

Delegates to the Constitutional Convention discuss the Virginia Plan in 1787.

Most people at the meeting liked the Virginia Plan. But it was still rough. From May to September, delegates talked about the plan.

This is the first page of the Virginia Plan.

They spent a long time figuring out how many Congress members each state would have. They decided the Senate would be made up of two people from each state. The House of Representatives would have at least one person from each state. Bigger states would have more House members than smaller states.

This painting shows the U.S. Senate meeting in the early 1830s. The Senate includes two people from each state.

A member of the
Constitutional
Convention signs the
new U.S. Constitution.

The delegates were tired after discussing the plan.
But they'd done their job. They'd made an outline for
running the country. They called it the U.S. Constitution.

Parts of the Constitution

The Constitution is four pages long. It has a preamble. That's an opening statement. Next are seven parts called articles.

The first three articles say government should have three parts. The parts are called branches. They are the executive branch, the legislative branch, and the judicial branch.

This is the first page of the Constitution. The entire Constitution is four pages.

The other articles outline the rest of the government. For example, they say a person doesn't have to be a certain religion to be a government official. They define the Constitution as the "supreme law of the land."

Benjamin Franklin was one of the signers of the Constitution. The signers are also called the founders.

The last paragraph says that only nine of the thirteen states had to agree to the Constitution before it went into effect. The Constitution didn't have to be ratified (approved) by each state's lawmakers. Instead, the states would hold conventions to ratify the Constitution. The people of each state would vote for convention delegates.

In less than a year, the people had voted for their delegates. The Constitution was ratified soon after.

This celebration took place in New York City after the Constitution was ratified.

Chapter 4

THE BILL OF RIGHTS

The Constitution almost wasn't ratified. In 1788, some states refused to ratify it if a bill of rights wasn't added. A bill of rights protects people from unjust rulers.

This document is the Bill of Rights. What does the Bill of Rights do?

George Washington was the first president under the new Constitution. He agreed that the Constitution should have a bill of rights. In 1789, at his swearing-in ceremony as president, he asked Congress to suggest amendments (additions) to the Constitution. Those amendments would make up a bill of rights.

George Washington (FIFTH FROM LEFT) **was sworn in as president in New York City in 1789.**

Ratified Rights

James Madison collected the amendments. The list was narrowed down to twelve. But the states ratified only ten of them. They were ratified in December 1791. They became the Bill of Rights.

THIS DRAFT SHOWS CHANGES THAT WERE MADE TO THE BILL OF RIGHTS BEFORE THE BILL WAS RATIFIED.

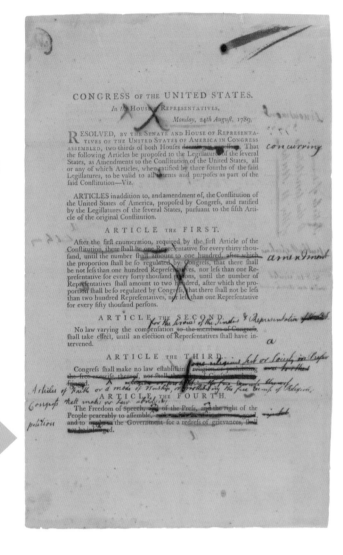

The Amendments

The First Amendment says Congress can't set up a state religion. It also says Congress can't pass laws that will make printers afraid to print the news. This right is called freedom of the press.

The Second Amendment says states need militias (people trained to fight). But the Third Amendment adds that people can't be forced to let troops live in their homes.

This illustration shows the British burning a newspaper in the 1730s. The First Amendment protects printers by giving them freedom of the press.

The Fourth Amendment says people have the right to feel safe at home. They shouldn't have to worry that their belongings will be searched or taken without a good reason.

British soldiers search a colonist's home without permission. The Fourth Amendment protects citizens from unreasonable searches.

The Fifth Amendment through the Eighth Amendment protect those accused of crimes. For example, they say Americans have a right to a trial.

The Sixth Amendment guarantees a trial by jury in public.

Americans celebrate their rights and freedoms on Independence Day in Riverton, New Jersey.

The last two amendments talk about what's not in the Constitution. The Ninth Amendment says that even if you don't see a right listed in the Constitution, it may still be protected. The Tenth Amendment says that when the Constitution doesn't give a specific power to the government, that power belongs to the states or to the people.

Road Maps

The Declaration, the Constitution, and the Bill of Rights are road maps to the U.S. government. The government they describe isn't perfect. But it has served our country for more than two hundred years.

The U.S. Capitol is the home of Congress. Congress is one part of the system of government set up by the Declaration, the Constitution, and the Bill of Rights.

Glossary

amendment: a change that is made to a law or a legal document. The first ten amendments to the Constitution are known as the Bill of Rights.

article: one of the seven original parts of the U.S. Constitution

colonist: a person who lives in a territory controlled by another country

colony: a territory that is controlled by another country

Congress: a group of elected officials who write, talk about, and make laws. The U.S. Congress is made up of the Senate and the House of Representatives.

delegate: someone who represents other people at a meeting

executive branch: the branch of government that is led by the president. The executive branch enforces the laws of the United States.

judicial branch: the branch of government involving the court system

legislative branch: the branch of government that makes laws

preamble: an opening statement

protest: to object to something strongly and publicly

ratify: to approve officially

rebellion: an armed fight against one's own government. Sometimes a rebellion is also called a revolution.

tax: money that people and businesses must pay to support a government

treaty: a formal agreement between two or more countries

Learn More about Government

Books

Landau, Elaine. *The Declaration of Independence*. New York: Children's Press, 2008. This book takes an interesting and thorough look at the Declaration of Independence.

Ransom, Candice. *George Washington and the Story of the U.S. Constitution*. Minneapolis: Millbrook Press, 2011. Learn more about the story behind George Washington and the Constitution in this fun book, which includes a Reader's Theater script for you to act out.

Roop, Connie, and Peter Roop. *The Top-Secret Adventure of John Darragh, Revolutionary War Spy*. Minneapolis: Graphic Universe, 2011. Young John Darragh helps his brother fight for freedom from Britain by sneaking messages to him. But his family lives across the street from the British army's headquarters. Will John get caught?

Stanton, Terence M. *The Bill of Rights: What It Means to You*. New York: Rosen Publishing Group, 2009. This book offers a clear explanation of the Bill of Rights as well as discussion questions for readers to explore.

Websites

Ben's Guide to U.S. Government for Kids
http://bensguide.gpo.gov/3-5/index.html
This website includes lots of useful information about the U.S. government.

Enchanted Learning: George Washington
http://www.enchantedlearning.com/history/us/pres/washington
Check out this page all about George Washington. You'll find a biography of Washington, a printout and quiz about him, a word search puzzle, and more.

Liberty! Road to Revolution Game
http://www.pbs.org/ktca/liberty/road.html
This fun and tricky quiz about the Revolutionary War is just right for students who feel up to an extra challenge!

Index

Photo Acknowledgments

The images in this book are used with the permission of: © Stock Montage/Archive Photos/Getty Images, p. 4; Library of Congress, pp. 5 (LC-DIG-ppmsca-15713), 13 (LC-USZ62-10658), 15 (LC-USZ62-55279), 17 (LC-USZC2-2243), 18 (LC-USZ62-49950), 22 (LC-DIG-ppmsca-19166), 28 (LC-DIG-ppmsca-10083); The Granger Collection, New York, pp. 6, 10, 11, 12, 25, 29; The Art Archive, p. 7; © Mary Evans Picture Library/The Image Works, p. 8; © North Wind Picture Archives, pp. 9, 16, 31, 33, 34; © Huntington Library/SuperStock, p. 14; National Archives, pp. 19, 21 (301687), 24 (5730363), 27, 30, 32 (3535588); © Three Lions/Hulton Archive/Getty Images, p. 20; Courtesy of the State Museum of Pennsylvania, Pennsylvania Historical and Museum Commission, John H. Froehlich, p. 23; © SuperStock/SuperStock, p. 26; © Ron Chapple/Taxi/Getty Images, p. 35; © Anthony Aneese Totah Jr/Dreamstime.com, p. 36; © fstockfoto/Dreamstime.com, p. 37.

Front cover: National Archives (top, middle, bottom); © Photodisc/Getty Images (background).

Main body text set in Adrianna Regular 14/20. Typeface provided by Chank.